Saudi Arabia

by Anastasiya Vasilyeva

Consultant: Marjorie Faulstich Orellana, PhD
Professor of Urban Schooling
University of California, Los Angeles

BEARPORT
PUBLISHING

New York, New York

Credits

Cover, © Arvind Balalraman/Shutterstock and © Fedor Selivanov/Shutterstock; TOC, © Beachboy/Alamy; 4, © Franckreporter/iStock; 5T, © Julien Garcia/Hemis/Alamy; 5B, © micheldenijs/iStock; 7, © Fitria Ramli/ Shutterstock; 8, © Giovanni Mereghetti/Marka/AGE Fotostock; 9, © brianeasley/iStock; 10T, © imageBROKER/Alamy; 10B, © SelimBT/Shutterstock; 11, © orestegaspari/iStock; 12, © Andrey Neksarov/AGE Fotostock; 13, © Matthew Taylor/Alamy; 14L, © The Stapleton Collection/Bridgeman Images; 14–15, © stefanoflorentino/iStock; 16, © Phillip Harrington/Alamy; 17, © Art Directors & Trips Photo/AGE Fotostock; 18, © Athar Akram/Alamy; 19, © age fotostock/ Alamy; 20, © oonal/iStock; 21, © Feije Riemersma/Alamy; 22, © B. O'Kane/Alamy; 22–23, © swisshippo/ iStock; 24, © David Kirkland/Axiom Photographic/AGE Fotostock; 25, © Photo 12/Alamy; 26, © AS Food Studio/ Shutterstock; 27, © PicturePartners/iStock; 28, © Ueslei Marcelino/Reuters/Newscom; 29T, © Hans Lippert/ imageBROKER/Alamy; 29B, © Stringer/Reuters/Newscom; 30T, © Ayed Moeed Al Jedaani/Dreamstime and © Fat Jackey/Shutterstock; 30B, © Badr Alzamil/Shutterstock; 31 (T to B), © Ali Al-Awartany/Shutterstock, © Vixit/ Shutterstock, © Barry Iverson/Alamy, and © oneinchpunch/Shutterstock; 32, © tulpahn/Shutterstock.

Publisher: Kenn Goin
Senior Editor: Joyce Tavolacci
Creative Director: Spencer Brinker
Design: Debrah Kaiser
Photo Researcher: Thomas Persano

Library of Congress Cataloging-in-Publication Data

Names: Vasilyeva, Anastasiya, author.
Title: Saudi Arabia / by Anastasiya Vasilyeva.
Description: New York, New York : Bearport Publishing Company, Inc., 2019. |
   Series: Countries we come from series | Includes bibliographical
   references.
Identifiers: LCCN 2018044150 (print) | LCCN 2018046119 (ebook) | ISBN
   9781642802672 (ebook) | ISBN 9781642801989 (library)
Subjects: LCSH: Saudi Arabia—Juvenile literature.
Classification: LCC DS204.25 (ebook) | LCC DS204.25 .V38 2019 (print) | DDC
   953.8—dc23
LC record available at https://lccn.loc.gov/2018044150

For more information, write to Bearport Publishing Company, Inc., 45 West 21st Street, Suite 3B, New York, New York 10010. Printed in the United States of America.

10 9 8 7 6 5 4 3 2 1

Contents

This Is Saudi Arabia

HOT

VAST

Modern

5

Saudi Arabia is a large country in the Middle East.

More than 28 million people live there!

Saudi Arabia is about three times bigger than Texas.

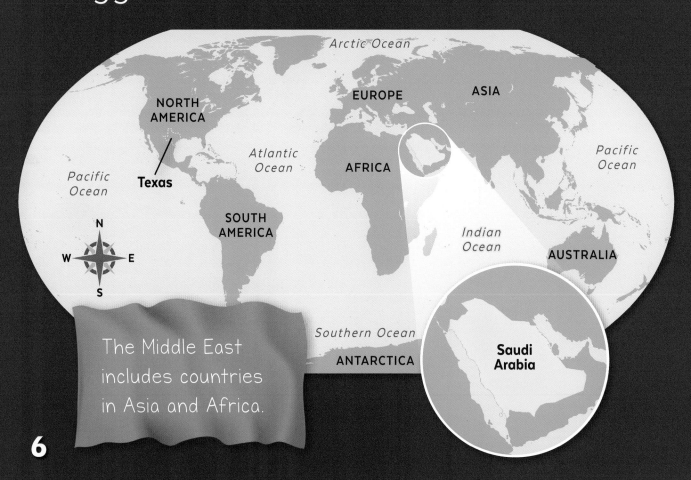

Arctic Ocean

NORTH AMERICA

EUROPE

ASIA

Atlantic Ocean

AFRICA

Texas

Pacific Ocean

Pacific Ocean

SOUTH AMERICA

N
W   E
S

Indian Ocean

AUSTRALIA

Southern Ocean

ANTARCTICA

Saudi Arabia

The Middle East includes countries in Asia and Africa.

7

Most of Saudi Arabia's land is hot, dry desert.

Saudi Arabia is the largest country in the world without a river!

The deserts are dotted with oases (oh-AY-seez).

An oasis is a place where plants and trees grow.

Oases get their water from underground springs.

Amazing animals live in Saudi Arabia.

Scorpions scurry across the sand.

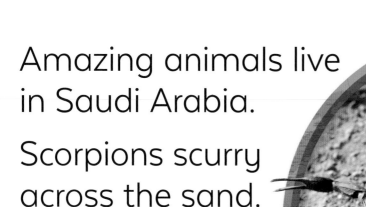

Desert owls soar in the sky.

Camels search for plants to eat.

Camels are made for harsh desert heat. They need very little water to survive.

People have lived in Saudi Arabia for thousands of years.

Nomads called Bedouins (BED-oh-ins) traveled from place to place.

They raised camels, sheep, and goats.

Bedouins often made their homes in big tents!

Today, small groups of nomads still live in the desert.

Bedouin tent

The people built towns that grew into cities.

One was called Mecca.

In 570, a man named Muhammad was born there.

He started a religion called Islam.

People who practice Islam are called Muslims. Today, Mecca is a holy city. All Muslims visit Mecca once in their lifetime.

After Muhammad died, different groups fought over the land.

In the 1900s, the Saud family **united** the country.

a Saudi king

Soon after, oil was discovered
in Saudi Arabia.

Saudi Arabia has more
oil than any other
country in the world!

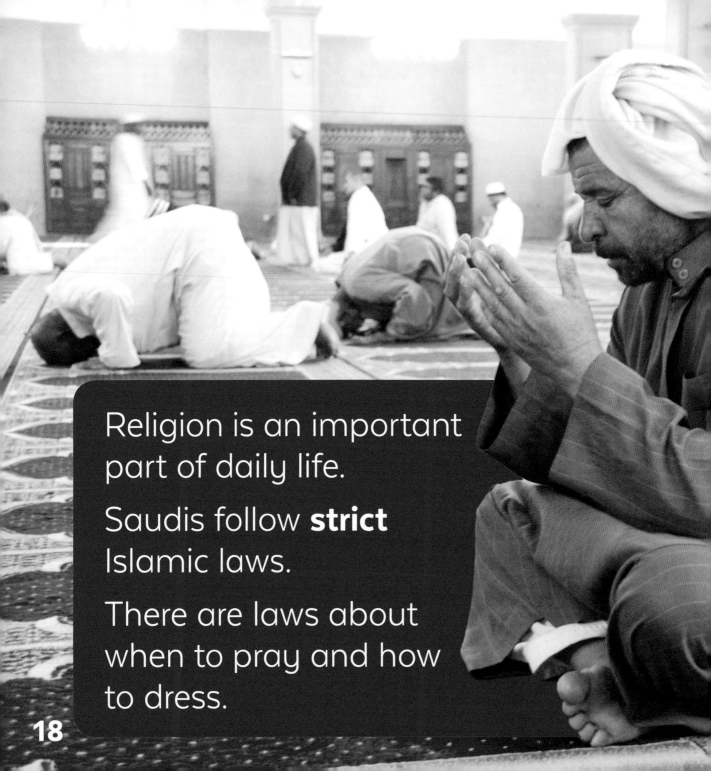

Religion is an important part of daily life.

Saudis follow **strict** Islamic laws.

There are laws about when to pray and how to dress.

18

The Koran is the sacred book of Islam.

Muslim people must pray five times each day.

19

What do people wear in Saudi Arabia?
Most women cover their hair with a scarf.
They wear long robes called abayas.
Many men also dress in long robes.

Many women also wear a *hijab*. It's a cloth that covers the face— but not the eyes.

21

Riyadh (ree-YADH) is the **capital** of Saudi Arabia.

It's also the country's largest city.

More than six million people live there.

a rug market in Riyadh

Most Saudi people live in cities.

Arabic is the main language of Saudi Arabia.

This is how you say *hello* in Arabic:

مرحبا

(MAR-ha-bah)

This is how you say *thank you*:

شكرا

(shoo-KRAN)

Many Saudi children learn English in school.

25

Saudi food is delicious.

Kabsa is a favorite dish.

It's spiced chicken and rice.

Yum!

Saudis love sweet fruits called dates. Dates and milk are often eaten for dessert.

What's the most popular sport in Saudi Arabia?

People love soccer.

Fans cheer for their favorite team!

peregrine falcon

Saudis enjoy falconry, too. They train birds called falcons to hunt.

Fast Facts

Capital city: Riyadh

Population of Saudi Arabia:
More than 28 million

Main language:
Arabic

Money: Saudi riyal

Major religion: Islam

Neighboring countries:
Bahrain, Iraq, Jordan, Kuwait, Oman,
Qatar, United Arab Emirates, and Yemen

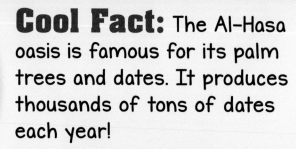

Cool Fact: The Al-Hasa
oasis is famous for its palm
trees and dates. It produces
thousands of tons of dates
each year!

Glossary

capital (KAP-uh-tuhl) the city where a country's government is based

nomads (NOH-madz) people who move from place to place

strict (STRIKT) demanding total obedience or observance

united (yoo-NITE-uhd) brought together

Index

Read More

Owings, Lisa. *Saudi Arabia (Exploring Countries).* Minnetonka, MN: Bellwether (2009).

Yomtov, Nel. *Saudi Arabia (Enchantment of the World).* New York: Scholastic (2014).

Learn More Online

To learn more about Saudi Arabia, visit
www.bearportpublishing.com/CountriesWeComeFrom

About the Author

Anastasiya Vasilyeva lives in New York City. She loves learning about new countries and trying different cuisines. One day soon, she hopes to taste Saudi food.